Muffin Mania.

by

Cathy Prange

and

Joan Pauli

Twentieth Printing

Published and Distributed by
Muffin Mania Publishing Ltd.,
553 Greenbrook Dr.,
Kitchener, Ontario.

Printed by Fairway Press
Kitchener, Ontario

Cover Photograph by Gail Shriber
Sketches by Marion Woeller

I.S.B.N.   0-9691485-0-X

Cathy Prange
Joan Pauli

Muffins - A Sign Of The Times
A Healthy Alternative To Junk Foods!

Every Friday morning is muffin baking time in our kitchens -- got to get ready for the week-end, you know! Well, after years and years of making the same old family favourites, we decided it was time for a change, so we searched through our books and magazines and started baking.

Naturally, we met with a few disasters in dry, hard, tasteless muffins. However, we weren't about to give up! Back to the kitchen we went. One by one we cut down on this, added a dash of that, and the result is the most mouth-watering collection of recipes that you can find.

You do not require a degree in Home Economics, and you need not attend a gourmet cooking class. Nothing could be simpler! These recipes are tried and proven through hours and hours of pure muffinery. Our families and friends can attest to each and every one of these recipes. We owe them a great deal of thanks for putting up with our muffin madness and other insanities, for what must have seemed like a thousand muffins. Also, a special thanks to our muffin-tasting gal friends who gave us great encouragement to put this collection together.

So gals, pull out your muffin tins,

turn the page to that muffin taste you always drooled for, and start baking. In fact, you'll get so excited with these muffin capers that you'll have them out of the oven before the gals come for 10:00 coffee!

The first thing you'll hear is... m-m-m-muffins!

Sisters, Partners and Friends,

Cathy Prange

Joan Pauli

Every muffin pictured on the cover is our mania and each recipe is in this book!

Hints

1. We used pre-sifted, all purpose flour. If using cake and pastry flour, you will need ¼ cup more.

2. Muffins, like tea biscuits, should be mixed as quickly and lightly as possible, only stirring to moisten. Batter should look lumpy. If using an electric mixer for blending, use only for the liquid ingredients.

3. We have baked most of our muffins at 375° as too hot an oven results in tough, leathery muffins. However, everyone's oven is different, so judge for yourself!

4. If you like big, beautiful muffins, fill tins to the top. Grease the top of the tins as well as the inside for easy unmolding.

5. If you have trouble unmolding fruit-filled muffins, let muffins cool completely before unmolding.

6. All these muffins freeze beautifully. To freeze, cool completely, wrap in foil and put in air-tight plastic bags. To reheat, unwrap and bake at 350° in oven or toaster oven. Soft, moist and hot - 10 min. Crusty - 15 min.

7. To sour milk or cream, add 1 tbsp. vinegar or lemon juice to 1 cup.

Never Serve A Cold Muffin!

Basic Muffin Batter

or

The Nothing Muffin

1 c. all purpose flour
2 tsp. baking powder
1/2 tsp. salt
1/2 c. sugar
1/2 c. milk
1/4 c. melted butter or margarine
1 egg

Stir together dry ingredients.

Add melted butter and beaten egg to milk.

Add liquid ingredients to dry, stirring only to moisten.

To this batter, add anything you have on the shelf - chocolate chips, butterscotch chips, peanut butter chips, fruit, nuts, etc.

or

Add nothing and serve with your scrambled eggs for breakfast with your favourite homemade jam or jelly.

Bake 375° - 15 or 20 min.

Yield - 8 medium muffins

Table Of Contents

Breakfast

Table of contents continued:

Table of contents continued:

Table of contents continued:

Dessert

Oh, by the way! While we have suggested different muffins for different times of the day, each one is perfect for any occasion, according to your taste.

Breakfast

Lorna's Apple Muffins

1/4 c. shortening or margarine
3/4 c. white sugar
1/2 tsp. vanilla
1 egg beaten
1 c. all purpose flour
1/2 tsp. baking soda
1 tsp. baking powder
1/4 tsp. salt
1/2 tsp. cinnamon
1/4 tsp. nutmeg
1 1/2 c. chopped apples
1 tbsp. cream

Cream shortening and sugar. Add vanilla and beaten egg.

Stir together dry ingredients and add, stirring just to moisten.

Add apples and cream gently.

Fill greased muffin cups and bake 350° for 20-25 min.

Apple Muffins without cheese are like a kiss without a squeeze! Why not try 1 cup of grated old cheddar in these?

Apple Cinnamon Muffins

1/2 c. butter or margarine
3/4 c. white sugar
1 egg beaten
1 c. buttermilk
1 tsp. salt
1 1/2 c. diced apple
1 c. all purpose flour
3/4 c. whole wheat flour
1 tsp. baking soda
1 tsp. cinnamon

Topping

1 tsp. cinnamon
2 - 3 tbsp. white sugar

Blend margarine, sugar, and egg until smooth.

Add buttermilk, salt, apples and mix well.

Stir together flour, soda, cinnamon and add stirring only to moisten.

Spoon into greased muffin cups and sprinkle with topping.

Bake 375° - 20 min.

Applesauce Bran Muffins

1 c. All Bran (cereal)
1/4 c. milk
1 c. applesauce
1/3 c. oil
1 egg
1 1/2 c. all purpose flour
3 tsp. baking powder
1/2 tsp. baking soda
1/2 tsp. salt
1 tsp. cinnamon
1/3 c. brown sugar

Stir All Bran, milk, applesauce, oil and egg together.

Stir together the dry ingredients.

Add bran mixture to dry ingredients, stirring just to moisten.

Bake 375° for 15 - 20 min.

Raisins or nuts, or both may be added to this batter.

3

Applesauce Oatmeal Muffins

1 c. all purpose flour
3 tsp. baking powder
1/2 tsp. cinnamon
1/2 tsp. salt
1/4 tsp. nutmeg
3/4 c. rolled oats
1/4 c. brown sugar
1 egg
1/4 c. oil
1/3 c. milk
2/3 c. applesauce

Mix dry ingredients well with a fork.

Beat egg, then add oil and milk.

Stir in applesauce.

Stir this into the dry ingredients, mixing only until moistened.

Spoon into greased muffin cups and bake 375° for 20 min.

Applesauce Raisin Muffins

4 eggs
2 c. white sugar
1 1/2 c. oil
1 3/4 c. applesauce
3 c. all purpose flour
1 tbsp. cinnamon
2 tsp. baking powder
2 tsp. baking soda
1 tsp. salt
2 c. raisins

Beat eggs slightly. Add sugar, oil and applesauce and beat thoroughly.

Add dry ingredients and blend until smooth.

Stir in raisins.

Fill greased muffin cups 2/3 full and sprinkle brown sugar on the top of batter.

Bake 375° for 15-20 min.

Best Ever Banana Muffins

3 large bananas
3/4 c. white sugar (½ c. sugar)
1 egg
1 tsp. baking soda
1 tsp. baking powder
1/2 tsp. salt
1 1/2 c. all purpose flour
1/3 c. melted butter or veg. oil.

Mash bananas. Add sugar and slightly beaten egg.

Add the melted butter.

Add the dry ingredients and bake 375° - 20 min.

This is our families' _very_ favourite!

Banana-Oatmeal Muffins

1 c. rolled oats
1 c. milk
2 c. all purpose flour   1½ c. wheat flour
1/2 c. white sugar   ¼ c. white ¼ c. bran
5 tsp. baking powder
1 tsp. baking soda
1 tsp. salt
1/2 tsp. cinnamon
1/4 tsp. nutmeg
1/2 c. margarine melted and cooled
2 eggs
2 tsp. vanilla
2 c. mashed bananas (4-5 med.)

Combine oats and milk and set aside.

In large bowl, mix flour, sugar, salt, baking powder, baking soda, cinnamon and nutmeg.

To soaked mixture, add melted margarine, eggs, vanilla and bananas.

Add wet mixture to dry ingredients and stir only until the flour is moistened.

Fill greased muffin cups and bake 375° - 20 min.

Whole Wheat Banana

Using whole wheat flour adds extra texture, flavour and fiber.

3/4 c. all purpose flour
3/4 c. whole wheat flour
1 tsp. baking soda
1 tsp. baking powder
1/2 tsp. salt
1/3 c. oil
2/3 c. brown sugar
2 eggs
1 c. mashed bananas (2-3 med.)

Topping

1/4 c. white sugar
1/2 tsp. cinnamon

Mash bananas. Combine bananas, brown sugar, oil and eggs. Beat until mixed.

Stir dry ingredients together and add to banana mixture, mixing to combine.

1/2 c. chopped nuts may be added to the batter.

Sprinkle topping on top of batter before baking.

Bake 350° - 20 min.

Crunchy Bran Muffins

1 c. buttermilk - *have substituted yogurt with success*
1 tsp. baking soda
1 c. all purpose flour
1/4 tsp. salt
1/2 c. butter or margarine
3/4 c. brown sugar *too sweet*
1 egg
1 tbsp. molasses *(I used honey)* †
1 c. bran - *we used natural bran*
1/4 c. each raisins or currants, finely chopped nuts and dates

Combine buttermilk and soda and set aside.

Cream butter and brown sugar thoroughly. Add egg and beat well.

Add buttermilk and soda, then molasses and bran and blend.

Stir in flour and salt mixture and fold in fruit and nuts.

Spoon into well-greased muffin cups and bake 375° - 20 min. or until done.

* I added 3 mashed bananas once, + it was a great success

This recipe was sent to us from our sister-in-law from the cottage country. It proved to be one of our favourite!

9

Honey Bran Muffins

1 c. natural bran
1 c. buttermilk
1/3 c. butter or margarine
1/2 c. brown sugar
2 tbsp. honey
1 egg
1 c. all purpose flour
2 tsp. baking powder
1/2 tsp. baking soda
1 tsp. salt

Soak bran in buttermilk while preparing the rest.

Cream butter and brown sugar. Beat in the honey and egg. Add the bran and buttermilk.

Stir together the flour, baking powder, baking soda, and salt.

Add dry ingredients and stir until moistened.

Bake 375° for 15-20 min.

Mother Milner's Old Fashioned Bran Muffins

Shortening the size of an egg (approx. 1/4 c.)

pinch of salt
3/4 c. brown sugar
1 egg
1 c. cooking bran
1/2 c. sour milk
1 scant tsp. baking soda
1 c. all purpose flour
1 tsp. baking powder

Cream shortening and sugar and add the egg and beat.

Add the bran and the sour milk in which the soda has been dissolved.

Add flour, baking powder and salt.

Bake 375° for 15-20 min.

Dates may be added. Cook the dates with a little water and let them cool. Mix the date mixture with flour before adding to batter.

As kids, we used to pour maple syrup over these for dessert -- m-m-good!

Mrs. Buns Bran Muffins

or

Pail Full Of Muffins

This recipe makes 6 doz. muffins.
The batter may be kept 6 weeks in the
refrigerator in a covered jar.

1 c. crisco or margarine
3 c. white sugar
3 tbsp. brown sugar
3 tbsp. baking soda
1 tbsp. salt
2 c. boiling water
2 c. 100% bran, coarse
5 c. all purpose flour
2 c. raisins or chopped dates
4 eggs
4 c. bran flakes (8 oz.)
1 qt. buttermilk

Pour water over 100% bran and let stand.

In very large bowl (or bath tub), cream
shortening, sugar and eggs. Add
buttermilk and then bran mixture. Stir
until blended.

Stir flour, soda, salt and add to above
mixture. Mix well.

Add bran flakes and fold in until just
moist. Add raisins or dates.

Chill 1 day before baking.

Bake 375° for 15-20 min.

Christmas Morning Cranberry Muffins

1 c. cranberries
1/4 c. white sugar
1 1/2 c. all purpose flour
1/4 c. white sugar
2 tsp. baking powder
1 tsp. salt
1/2 tsp. cinnamon
1/4 tsp. ground all spice
1 beaten egg
1/4 tsp. grated orange peel
3/4 c. orange juice
1/3 c. melted butter or margarine
1/4 c. chopped walnuts

Coarsely chop cranberries.

Sprinkle with 1/4 c. sugar and set aside.

In bowl, stir together flour, 1/4 c. sugar, baking powder, salt, cinnamon, all spice and make a well in the centre.

Combine egg, orange peel, orange juice and melted butter. Add all at once to the flour mixture stirring to moisten.

Fold in cranberry mixture and nuts.

Fill greased muffin cups and bake 375° for 15-20 min. or until golden.

Date Muffins

1 c. chopped dates
1 tsp. baking soda
1/4 c. margarine or shortening

Pour 1 c. boiling water over this and let cool.

Add 1 small cup brown sugar to one well-beaten egg and add to cooled date mixture.

Add 1 c. bran
    1 tsp. baking powder
    1 c. all purpose flour

Stir to moisten.

Bake 375° for 15-20 min.

Sonja's Date Muffins

Very Moist

1/2 c. brown sugar
1 egg
1 tsp. salt
1 tbsp. melted shortening
1 c. date filling
1 1/2 c. bran
3/4 c. all purpose flour
1 tsp. baking soda
1 c. sour milk or buttermilk

Date Filling

1 c. chopped dates
1 c. hot water
1/2 c. brown sugar
1 tsp. lemon juice
Mix and simmer until thickened.

Method

Measure sugar, egg, salt, shortening and date filling into bowl. Beat vigorously until smooth.

Add bran.

Add flour and baking soda, then milk. Stir only to moisten ingredients.

Spoon into greased muffin cups and let stand three minutes.

Bake 375° – 20 min.

15

Health Food Muffins

1 1/4 c. all purpose flour
2 tsp. baking powder
2 c. granola
1/4 c. brown sugar
1 tsp. salt
1/3 c. oil
1 c. milk
1 tsp. vanilla
1/3 c. molasses

Mix together dry ingredients.

Blend oil, milk, vanilla and molasses.

Pour mixture over dry ingredients and stir only to moisten.

Spoon into well-greased muffin cups, sprinkling more granola on the top.

Bake 375° for 15-20 min.

Marmalade Muffins

Light, bittersweet — a real hit for breakfast or coffee break!

Peel of 1 grapefruit and 1 orange
1 1/2 c. buttermilk
1 c. white sugar
1 tsp. salt
1/2 c. margarine
1 3/4 c. all purpose flour
2 tsp. baking powder
1/2 tsp. baking soda

Cut complete grapefruit and orange skins into blender.

Pour in buttermilk and grind fine.

Add sugar, salt and shortening and blend.

Stir dry ingredients together in a bowl and pour rind mixture over, stirring just to moisten flour.

Bake 375° - 20 min.

For a slightly sweeter taste, while warm, dip in melted butter and white sugar. Absolutely scrumptious!

Oatmeal Muffins

1 c. oatmeal
1 c. boiling water

Mix and let stand 20 min.

1 1/2 c. brown sugar (or less)
1/2 c. butter or margarine
2 eggs well beaten
1 tsp. baking soda
1 tsp. salt
1 tsp. vanilla
1 c. all purpose flour
3/4 c. dates cut fine   or 1 c. raisins

Cream sugar and butter.

Add eggs and beat.

Add the dates to the dry ingredients and add.

Add vanilla.

Stir in oatmeal mixture gently.

Bake 375° for 20-25 min.

A handful of coconut added to this batter makes a nice variation.

Oatmeal Orange Muffins

1 c. oats soaked in 1/2 c. orange juice
1/2 c. boiling water
for 15 min.

1/2 c. margarine
1/2 c. white sugar
1/2 c. brown sugar
2 eggs beaten
1 c. raisins
1 c. all purpose flour
1 tsp. baking powder
1 tsp. baking soda
1 tsp. salt
1 tsp. vanilla

Cream margarine and sugar. Beat in eggs and stir in oat mixture. Stir in raisins.

Add flour, baking powder, baking soda, salt and vanilla.

Stir until moistened. Pour into well-greased muffin cups.

Bake 350° – 20 min.

Pioneer Muffins

This is a very moist, health food muffin. Makes 2 doz. muffins.

3 eggs
1/3 c. brown sugar
2/3 c. vegetable oil
1/4 c. molasses
2 c. natural bran
1 c. grated carrots
1 c. applesauce, mashed bananas, or pureed fruit
1 1/2 c. liquid (water, milk or apple juice)
1 1/2 c. whole wheat flour
1/2 c. wheat germ
1 tsp. baking soda
2 tsp. baking powder
1 tsp. salt
1 tbsp. powdered milk
1/2 c. raisins (optional)

If using applesauce, add 2 tsp. cinnamon to dry ingredients and 1 c. chopped walnuts.

Method

In large bowl, beat eggs. Add sugar, oil, molasses, bran, carrot, applesauce and liquid. Stir well.

In medium bowl, mix well whole wheat flour, wheat germ, soda, baking powder, salt, powdered milk and raisins.

Add dry ingredients all at once to egg mixture, stirring only until moistened.

Bake 375° for 20-25 min.

Auntie Thelma's Whole Wheat Muffins

1 egg well beaten
1 scant cup brown sugar
1/2 tsp. salt
1 tsp. vanilla

Beat all this together and then add:

1 c. sour cream - not commercial, sour
your own with vinegar
or lemon juice
1 c. whole wheat flour
1 tsp. baking powder
1 scant tsp. baking soda

Fill greased muffin cups and bake
375° for 10-15 min.

Coffee Break

Apricot-Oatmeal Muffins

1 1/4 c. rolled oats (regular or
                        instant)
1 c. all purpose flour
1/3 c. granulated sugar
1 tbsp. baking powder
1/2 tsp. salt
2/3 c. milk
1 - 4 1/2 oz. jar apricot puree (baby
                        food)
1 egg
1/4 c. oil
1 tsp. vanilla
1/2 c. chopped dried apricots
1/3 c. raisins

Measure first five ingredients in large
bowl and mix well.

Mix milk, apricot puree, egg, oil, and
vanilla in another bowl.

Add wet ingredients to dry and stir just
until moistened.

Fold in apricots and raisins.

Fill greased muffin cups 2/3 full and
bake 350° - 20 min.

Carrot Nut Muffins

1 c. white sugar
3/4 c. oil
2 eggs
1 tsp. baking soda dissolved in 1 tbsp.
      warm water
1/2 tsp. salt
1 tsp. baking powder
1 tsp. vanilla
1 1/2 c. all purpose flour
1 c. walnuts
1 c. grated carrots

Beat sugar, oil, and eggs.

Add baking soda and water and vanilla.
Mix well.

Add flour, salt and baking powder and
mix until moistened.

Stir in grated carrots and nuts.

Bake 375° for 15-20 min.

Also good with currants, raisins,
quartered maraschino cherries, orange
or lemon rind or cut peel. Your
left-over Christmas fruit is ideal!

Carrot Pineapple Muffins

1 c. white sugar
2/3 c. oil
2 large eggs beaten
1 1/2 c. all purpose flour
2 tsp. baking powder
1 tsp. baking soda
1 tsp. cinnamon
1/2 tsp. salt
1 tsp. vanilla
1 c. finely grated carrot
1 c. crushed pineapple drained

In beater bowl, combine sugar, oil and beaten eggs.

In another bowl, combine flour, baking powder, baking soda, cinnamon and salt and mix well.

Add dry ingredients to the sugar and oil mixture and stir to moisten.

Add grated carrots, pineapple and vanilla.

Fill greased muffin cups to the top and bake 375° - 20 min.

Chopped nuts may be added if desired.

Carrot Wheat Muffins

1 c. all purpose flour
1/2 c. whole wheat flour
2 tsp. baking powder
1/2 tsp. salt
1/4 c. brown sugar
1/2 tsp. cinnamon
1/8 tsp. allspice
1 c. carrots, coarsely grated
1 tsp. grated orange rind
1 egg
1 c. milk
1/4 c. molasses
1/4 c. melted butter
1/2 c. raisins
1/4 c. chopped nuts

Measure dry ingredients in large bowl.

Stir in carrots and orange rind.

In small bowl, beat egg with milk, molasses and melted butter.

Add to dry ingredients all at once, stirring just to moisten.

Fold in raisins and nuts.

Fill greased muffin cups 3/4 full.

Bake 375° - 20 min.

Honey-Carrot-Date Muffins

1/4 c. butter or margarine
1/2 c. honey
1/2 c. milk
2 eggs
1 1/2 c. all purpose flour
1 heaping tsp. baking powder
1 tsp. salt
1 c. grated carrots (2 med. carrots)
1 c. pitted, chopped dates

Melt butter and honey. Stir in eggs and milk and beat.

Combine dry ingredients and stir thoroughly.

Stir in liquid mixture and fold in carrots and dates.

Bake 375° - 15-20 min.

Delicious when heated and served with butter, cream cheese or marmalade!

Coffee-Date Muffins

1 c. dates chopped
2/3 c. strong, hot coffee
1/2 tsp. cinnamon
2/3 c. shortening or margarine
1 c. brown sugar
2 eggs
1 1/2 c. all purpose flour
1 tsp. baking powder
1/2 tsp. baking soda
1/2 tsp. salt

Combine dates, cinnamon and coffee and let stand 20 min. to soften dates.

Cream shortening, sugar, and add 1 egg at a time and beat.

Add date mixture.

Mix dry ingredients together and add, stirring just to moisten.

Bake 375° - 20 min.

Ice with 1/2 c. icing sugar
        1 tbsp. coffee
        when slightly cooled.

Coffee Walnut Muffins

1 tbsp. instant coffee
1/2 c. hot water
1/2 c. whole milk or cream
1 egg beaten
1/2 c. melted shortening or oil
1 1/2 c. all purpose flour
3 tsp. baking powder
1/3 c. white sugar
1 tsp. salt
1/2 c. chopped walnuts

Dissolve coffee in hot water and add the cream, beaten egg and shortening.

Stir flour, baking powder, salt and sugar together and stir in the walnuts.

Pour liquid ingredients into the dry and mix only to moisten.

Spoon into greased muffin cups and bake 375° for 15-20 min.

Gingersnap Raisin Muffins

1/4 c. margarine
1/4 c. white sugar
1 egg
1/2 c. molasses
1 c. all purpose flour
1 tsp. baking soda
1/4 tsp. salt
1/2 tsp. cinnamon
1/2 tsp. ginger
1/4 tsp. cloves
1/2 c. hot water
1 c. raisins

Cream margarine and sugar. Add egg and molasses and beat.

Stir together flour, baking soda, salt, cinnamon, ginger and cloves.

Stir into molasses mixture and gradually add the hot water and stir until smooth.

Stir in raisins which have been plumped in hot water and squeezed dry.

Fill greased muffin cups and bake 375° for 20 min.

Morning Glory Muffins

Into a large bowl mix:

2 c. all purpose flour
1 1/4 c. white sugar
2 tsp. baking soda
2 tsp. cinnamon
1/2 tsp. salt

Stir in:

2 c. grated carrot
1/2 c. raisins
1/2 c. nuts
1/2 c. coconut
1 apple, peeled, cored and grated

In bowl, beat 3 eggs
            1 c. salad oil
            2 tsp. vanilla

Stir into flour mixture until batter is just combined.

Spoon into well greased muffin cups, filling to the top.

Bake 350° - 20 min. Makes about 14 large, scrumptious muffins!

Aunt Dorothy raved about these! She thought we should call them, "Heavenly Hash"!

Orange-Date Muffins

1 whole orange
1/2 c. orange juice
1/2 c. chopped dates
1 egg
1/2 c. butter or margarine
1 1/2 c. all purpose flour
1 tsp. baking soda
1 tsp. baking powder
1/2 tsp. salt
3/4 c. white sugar

Cut the orange into pieces to remove seeds.

Drop pieces into blender with 1/2 c. orange juice and whirl until peel is finely chopped.

Drop in the dates, egg and butter. Give blender a short whirl.

Stir together the dry ingredients.

Pour orange mixture over and stir only until moistened.

Bake 375° for 15-20 min.

Raisins may be substituted for the dates for an equally delicious muffin.

Dallas's Oatmeal Carrot Muffins

1 c. buttermilk
1 c. quick-cooking oats (not instant)
1 egg beaten
1/2 c. brown sugar
1/3 c. melted butter or margarine
1 c. finely shredded carrots
1 tsp. vanilla
    grated rind of 1 orange
1 c. whole wheat or all purpose flour
2 tsp. baking powder
1 tsp. baking soda
1 tsp. salt

Pour buttermilk over oats in bowl.
Add beaten egg, melted butter,
sugar, carrots, vanilla and orange
rind and mix thoroughly.

Combine flour, baking powder,
baking soda, and salt and mix.
Add to oat mixture stirring just
until moistened.

If desired, add raisins or dates
at this point.

Fill greased muffin cups.

Bake 375° for 15 - 20 min.

33

Peanut Butter Muffins

Super for the little folk!

1 1/2 c. all purpose flour
1/2 c. white sugar
2 tsp. baking powder
1/2 tsp. salt
1/2 c. chunky peanut butter
1/4 c. butter
1 c. milk
2 beaten eggs

Mix dry ingredients and cut in peanut butter and butter until mixture is crumbly.

Add eggs and milk and stir until moistened.

Fill greased muffin cups and sprinkle with mixture of chopped peanuts and sugar.

Or

After baking, while hot, brush tops with melted jelly and dip in chopped peanuts.

Bake 375° for 15-20 min.

Pumpkin Muffins

4 eggs
2 c. white sugar   *coconut palm sugar*
1 1/2 c. oil   *organic coconut oil*
1 3/4 c. pumpkin (small can)
3 c. all purpose flour
1 tbsp. cinnamon   *cardoman*
2 tsp. baking powder
2 tsp. baking soda
1 tsp. salt
2 c. raisins   *HEMP SEEDS*

Beat eggs slightly. Add sugar, oil, pumpkin and beat thoroughly.

Add dry ingredients and mix until smooth.

Stir in raisins.

Fill greased muffin cups 2/3 full and sprinkle tops with brown sugar.

Bake 375° for 15-20 min.

This is a good Fall muffin for Octoberfest or Thanksgiving!

use mixmaster

Raisin Muffins

3/4 c. brown sugar
1/2 c. shortening or margarine
1 1/4 c. raisins washed
1 egg
1 1/4 c. all purpose flour
1 tsp. nutmeg
1 tsp. baking soda
1/2 tsp. salt

Cream sugar and shortening. Add egg and beat until fluffy.

Cook raisins in 2 c. water for 20 min. Drain raisins saving 1/2 c. liquid.

Add liquid to creamed mixture.

Stir dry ingredients together and add to above stirring until moistened.

Stir in cooked raisins.

Bake 375° for 15-20 min.

Lunch – Brunch

Muffins Instead Of Bread

Donna's Beer Muffins

Another Octoberfest muffin! Serve with traditional German food - cabbage rolls, pig tails, etc.

3 c. all purpose flour
5 tsp. baking powder
1/2 tsp. salt
3 tbsp. white sugar
1 bottle of beer

Measure dry ingredients into bowl and pour beer over, stirring to blend.

Spoon into greased muffin cups and brush tops with butter.

Bake 350° for 15-20 min.

Serve hot! A little grated cheddar cheese sprinkled on top of these before baking makes them even better!

Cheddar Cornmeal Muffins

1 c. all purpose flour
1/2 c. corn meal
1 heaping tsp. baking powder
1/2 tsp. salt
    pinch cayenne
1 c. milk
1 egg
1/4 c. melted butter or margarine
1 1/2 c. grated sharp cheddar cheese

Stir together flour, corn meal, baking powder, salt and cayenne.

Beat egg with milk and butter and add to dry ingredients stirring to moisten.

Stir in 1 c. cheese and spoon into greased muffin cups. Sprinkle with remaining cheese.

Bake 375° for 15-20 min.

Serve hot with butter or freeze and reheat before serving. These are delicious with homemade soups, chili, or salads. For a yummy variation, add 1/2 c. cooked, crumbled bacon to the batter. Makes 8 large muffins.

Cornmeal Muffins

An old fashioned Waterloo County favourite.

1 c. flour
1 tbsp. baking powder
1/2 tsp. salt
1/2 c. white sugar
1 c. cornmeal
1/2 c. butter or margarine
1 egg
3/4 c. milk

Mix dry ingredients together and stir in cornmeal.

Melt butter, add egg and milk and combine well.

Stir liquid ingredients into dry and combine just until moistened.

Fill greased muffin cups and bake 375° for 15-20 min.

Serve hot!

Variation: Add 1/2 c. corn niblets or
1/2 c. crumbled bacon.

Bacon-Corn Muffins

1/2 lb. bacon
1 c. all purpose flour
1 c. cornmeal
2 tbsp. sugar
1 tbsp. baking powder
1/2 tsp. salt
1 - 10 oz. can cream corn
1/2 c. milk
1 egg beaten

Cook bacon until brown and crisp. Drain on paper towel and crumble. Set aside. Reserve 1/4 c. bacon fat.

Mix flour, cornmeal, sugar, baking powder and salt.

In small bowl, beat corn, milk, egg and bacon dripping.

Stir into flour mixture and fold in bacon pieces.

Bake 375° for 15-20 min. or until done.

Serve Warm!

Cheese Bran Muffins

1 c. whole bran
1 1/2 c. sour milk or buttermilk
1/4 c. margarine
1/4 c. white sugar
1 egg
1 1/2 c. all purpose flour
2 tsp. baking powder
1/2 tsp. salt
1/4 tsp. baking soda
1 c. shredded old cheddar cheese

Soak bran in sour milk.

Cream margarine and sugar. Beat in egg.

Stir together dry ingredients and add to creamed mixture alternately with the bran, starting and ending with flour mixture.

Stir in cheese.

Fill greased muffin cups and bake 375° for 20-30 min.

Serve warm!

Cheese and Ginger Muffins

1 1/2 c. all purpose flour
2 tsp. baking powder
1/2 tsp. baking soda
1 tsp. ground ginger
1/2 tsp. salt
    dash cayenne
1 egg
1/2 c. milk
1/2 c. corn syrup
1/4 c. margarine
1 c. grated old cheddar cheese

Mix dry ingredients in bowl.

Melt margarine. Add beaten egg, milk and corn syrup and mix well. Combine dry ingredients with egg mixture and mix until moistened.

Stir in grated cheese.

Fill greased muffin cups and bake 375° for 15-20 min.

If desired, sprinkle tops with more grated cheese before baking.

Serve <u>hot</u>!

Cheese and Onion Muffins

1 1/2 c. all purpose flour
1 tbsp. baking powder
1 tbsp. white sugar
1/4 tsp. salt (OMIT)
1 c. shredded old cheddar cheese
1 pkg. onion soup mix
1 c. milk
1 egg
1/4 c. oil

Stir together dry ingredients and stir in the cheese.

Combine soup mix and milk. Let stand 5 min.

Beat egg, milk mixture and oil and add to dry ingredients mixing lightly just to combine.

Spoon into well greased muffin cups and bake 375° for 15-20 min.

Serve hot!

These were a big hit at our muffin Tasting Luncheon!

43

Mushroom Muffins

1 egg
1/3 c. melted shortening or oil
1/4 c. milk
1 can (10 oz.) condensed cream of
                mushroom soup (undiluted)
1 1/2 c. all purpose flour
3 tsp. baking powder
1/4 tsp. salt
2 tbsp. cut up parsley or chives (optional

Beat the egg and blend in shortening, milk and soup.

Stir together flour, baking powder and salt.

Add the liquid ingredients to the dry along with parsley or chives, stirring only until moistened.

Bake 375° for 15-20 min.

Serve warm!

We don't know why you couldn't make these with any tin of cream soup. Try them with a mary for a morning eye opener!

44

Sandy's Sea-Food Muffins

1 c. small shrimp drained and coarsely
    chopped
1/4 c. shredded old cheddar cheese
1/3 c. sour cream
1/4 c. finely chopped celery

1 1/2 c. all purpose flour
2 tbsp. white sugar
2 tsp. baking powder
1/2 tsp. salt
1/4 tsp. thyme

1 egg
3/4 c. milk
1/3 c. oil
parsley

Combine shrimp, cheese, sour cream and
celery. Set aside.

In bowl, stir flour, sugar, baking powder,
salt and thyme.

Make a well in centre of dry ingredients.

In bowl, slightly beat the egg with a
fork, beat in milk and oil. Add to dry
ingredients and stir just until moist.

Spoon into well greased muffin cups and
top with the shrimp mixture - about 1 tbsp.

Bake 375o - 20 min. Garnish with snipped
parsley if desired. Serve warm.
Delicious! For a more economical muffin,
try tuna or salmon instead of shrimp.

Blueberry Muffins

1 3/4 c. all purpose flour
1/2 c. white sugar
3 tsp. baking powder
1 c. milk
1/2 c. melted butter
1 egg
1/2 tsp. salt
1 c. frozen blueberries

Stir together dry ingredients and add frozen blueberries.

Combine egg, milk and melted butter and stir into flour mixture and blueberries stirring just to moisten. Do not beat.

Bake 375° - 20 min.

For a nice flavour, add the gratec rind of one orange or lemon and while hot, dip in melted butter and sugar.

Blueberry Oatmeal Muffins

1 c. all purpose flour
2 tsp. baking powder try 3 tsp. B.P.
1/2 tsp. salt
1/2 tsp. cinnamon
3/4 c. rolled oats
1/2 c. lightly packed brown sugar
1 egg
1 c. milk
1/4 c. melted margarine
3/4 c. fresh or frozen blueberries

Stir dry ingredients together. Add
sugar and rolled oats.

Beat together in large bowl, egg, milk
and melted margarine.

Add the dry ingredients and stir just
until moistened.

Fold in blueberries.

Bake 375° for 20 min. or until brown.

This recipe was sent to us from a
friend from the West. She uses
Saskatoon Berries. We think elderberries
or any other local fruit in season would
be delicious.

The 2nd time I made these they
were a disaster!
3rd time - o.k. - they didn't rise much, tho'
Added some raisins, & that was good. But warm them!

Tea Time

Cherry Muffins

1 1/2 c. all purpose flour
1/2 c. white sugar
2 tsp. baking powder
1/2 tsp. salt
3 tbsp. melted butter
2 eggs
1 c. cherry juice and milk combined
1/2 small bottle maraschino cherries
    cut up.

Stir together dry ingredients and add the cherries.

Mix eggs, milk and cherry juice (1/2 and 1/2) and melted butter.

Stir the liquid ingredients into the flour mixture stirring just to moisten.

Bake 375° for 15-20 min.

Joye's Lemon Tea Muffins

1 c. all purpose flour
1/2 c. sugar
1 heaping tsp. baking powder
1 tsp. salt
1/4 c. melted butter
1/2 c. fresh lemon juice
2 eggs
    finely grated lemon rind (1 lemon)

Combine dry ingredients and blend well.

Melt butter. Remove from heat and stir in lemon juice, eggs and lemon rind.

Stir egg mixture into dry ingredients and stir only to moisten.

Bake 375° for 15-20 min. until nicely browned.

Remove from pan while warm and dip in topping.

Topping

1/4 c. melted butter
1 tbsp. lemon juice
1/2 c. white sugar

Combine melted butter and lemon juice. Measure sugar in separate dish. Dunk top of muffins into butter, then sugar.

A cup of raisins added to this batter makes this a pleasurable muffin for any time of the day.

Lemonade Muffins

1 1/2 c. all purpose flour
1/4 c. white sugar
2 1/2 tsp. baking powder
1/2 tsp. salt
1 beaten egg
1 - 6 oz. can (2/3 cup) frozen lemonade
          thawed
1/4 c. milk
1/3 c. cooking oil
1/2 c. chopped walnuts

Mix dry ingredients.

Combine egg, 1/2 c. lemonade, milk and oil.

Add to dry ingredients and stir just until moistened.

Gently stir in nuts.

Fill greased muffin cups and bake 375° for 15-20 min. or until done.

While hot, brush with remaining lemonade and sprinkle with white sugar.

Maple Walnut Muffins

Harry's Favourite

1 c. all purpose flour
1/2 c. whole wheat flour
2 tsp. baking powder
1 tsp. salt
1/2 tsp. cinnamon
1/4 c. butter or margarine
1/3 c. pure maple syrup
2/3 c. milk
1 egg
1/2 tsp. maple extract
1/2 c. chopped walnuts

In bowl, combine dry ingredients except nuts.

Melt butter. Add syrup and milk, then beat in egg and maple extract.

Stir butter mixture into dry ingredients and stir to moisten.

Stir in walnuts.

Sprinkle tops of muffin batter with sugar-nut topping.

Bake 375° for 15-20 min.

Sugar-Nut Topping

Combine 2 tbsp. sugar with
1/4 tsp. cinnamon and
3 tbsp. finely chopped nuts

These would also be delicious using pecans instead of walnuts.

52

Muffins That Taste Like Donuts

1 3/4 c. all purpose flour
1 1/2 tsp. baking powder
1/2 tsp. salt
1/2 tsp. nutmeg
1/4 tsp. cinnamon
1/3 c. oil
3/4 c. white sugar (first amount)
1 egg
3/4 c. milk

1/2 c. melted butter
3/4 c. white sugar (second amount)
1 tsp. cinnamon

In a bowl combine flour, baking powder, salt, nutmeg and cinnamon.

In another bowl combine thoroughly oil, sugar, egg and milk.

Add liquid ingredients to dry and stir only to combine.

Bake 350° for 20-25 min.

Shake muffins out immediately and while hot, dip in melted butter, then sugar and cinnamon.

For a delicious variation, fill tins 1/2 full of batter, put 1 tsp. jam on top, and top with the rest of the batter.

Rich Delicious Orange Tea Muffins

1 1/2 c. all purpose flour
1/2 c. white sugar
2 tsp. baking powder
1/2 tsp. salt
1/2 c. butter or margarine melted
1/2 c. fresh orange juice
2 eggs
   grated rind of 1 orange

Combine flour, sugar, baking powder, and salt and blend well.

Melt butter. Take off heat and stir in orange juice, eggs and orange rind. Beat.

Stir liquid into dry mixture and blend just until moistened.

Spoon into greased muffin cups and soak 1 sugar cube in orange juice and place on top of batter.

Bake 375° for 15-20 min. or until done.

A handful of coconut or raisins added to this batter would also be delicious!

Sour Cream Muffins

1 egg
1 c. sour cream
1/4 c. milk
1 1/2 c. all purpose flour
2 tbsp. sugar
1 tsp. baking powder
1/2 tsp. baking soda
1 tsp. nutmeg
1 tsp. salt
1/2 c. raisins (if desired)

Beat egg. Stir in sour cream and milk.

Stir dry ingredients together and blend into batter.

Fold in raisins and spoon into well greased muffin cups.

Bake 375° for 15-20 min.

Sour Cream-Pineapple Muffins

1/4 c. white sugar
1 egg
1/4 c. butter or margarine (soft)
1 c. dairy sour cream
1 1/2 c. all purpose flour
1 tsp. baking powder
1/2 tsp. baking soda
1/2 tsp. salt
1 c. well-drained, crushed pineapple

Measure sugar, egg, soft butter and sour cream into bowl and beat.

Stir together flour, baking powder, baking soda and salt and blend.

Add cream mixture to dry ingredients and stir until moistened.

Stir in pineapple to mix.

Fill greased muffin cups and bake 375° for 15-20 min.

Muffins For Dessert

Why Not?

Chocolate Cheesecake Muffins

1 - 3 oz. pkg. cream cheese
2 tbsp. granulated sugar
1 c. all purpose flour
1/2 c. sugar
3 tbsp. unsweetened cocoa powder
2 tsp. baking powder
1/2 tsp. salt
1 beaten egg
3/4 c. milk
1/3 c. cooking oil
    powdered sugar

In small bowl, beat cream cheese and 2 tbsp. sugar until light and fluffy. Set aside.

In large bowl, stir together flour, 1/2 c. sugar, cocoa, baking powder, and salt.

Make a well in centre of dry ingredients. Combine egg, milk and oil. Add all at once to dry ingredients stirring just until moistened. (Batter should be lumpy).

Spoon about 2 tbsp. of chocolate batter into each greased muffin cup or paper cup. Drop 1 tsp. of cream cheese on top and then more chocolate batter.

Bake 375° - 20 min.

Dust with powdered sugar if desired.

Our friend, Fanny, a chocolate "nut", liked these best of all!

mmm!

Chocolate Chip Muffins

1 1/2 c. all purpose flour
1/2 c. white sugar
3 tsp. baking powder
1/4 tsp. salt
1 c. milk
1/3 c. melted butter
1 egg
1 c. chocolate chips

Mix dry ingredients and add chocolate chips.

Combine egg, milk and butter and stir into flour mixture. Do not beat.

Bake 375° - 20 min.

A few chocolate chips melted and drizzled over the tops when slightly cooled, make these a special dessert treat for chocolate lovers.

Our Cadet, Bob, from Robert Land Academy, always requests these when he's home on week-end leaves.

Jam Filled Muffins

1 1/2 c. all purpose flour
1/4 c. white sugar
2 tsp. baking powder
1/2 tsp. baking soda
1/2 tsp. salt
1/4 c. butter or margarine
1 c. plain yogurt
1/4 c. milk
1 egg
1/2 tsp. vanilla
    jam or jelly

Blend dry ingredients.

Melt butter. Take off heat and stir in yogurt and milk and blend. Beat in egg and vanilla.

Add butter mixture to dry ingredients and stir until moistened.

Spoon half of the batter into well-greased muffin cups. Place about 1 tsp. raspberry jam or jam or jelly of your choice in each muffin and top with remaining batter.

Bake 375° - 15-20 min.

Dust with confectioner's sugar before serving if desired.

Maple Syrup Muffins (Heavenly)

1/4 c. margarine
1/2 c. white sugar
1 tsp. salt
1 1/4 c. all purpose flour
2 tsp. baking powder
3/4 c. rolled oats
1/2 c. milk
1/2 c. maple syrup

Glaze

1 tbsp. butter
1/2 c. icing sugar
1 tbsp. maple syrup

Soften margarine, blend in sugar and salt.

Add dry ingredients and blend with pastry cutter until crumbly. Mix in oats.

Blend milk and syrup together in measuring cup and pour over dry ingredients stirring only to moisten.

Bake 350° - 20 min.

Spread glaze over when slightly cooled.

Mincemeat Rum Muffins

1 1/2 c. all purpose flour
1/4 c. white sugar
2 tsp. baking powder
1/2 tsp. salt
1/2 c. margarine melted
1/2 c. apple juice
2 eggs
1 c. mincemeat (canned)

Combine dry ingredients and blend well.

Melt margarine and stir in apple juice and eggs. Beat well.

Stir liquid ingredients into dry mixture.

Add mincemeat and stir until moistened.

Spoon into greased muffin cups and soak 1 sugar cube in rum and place on top of batter.

Bake 375° for 15 - 20 min.

A delicious muffin for the Christmas Season!

Pina Colada Muffins

1/2 c. white sugar
1 egg
1/4 c. margarine
1 c. sour cream
1 tsp. rum extract
1 1/2 c. all purpose flour
1 tsp. baking powder
1/2 tsp. baking soda
1/2 tsp. salt
1 small can drained crushed pineapple
1/2 c. coconut

Measure sugar, egg, margarine, sour cream and rum extract and beat until blended.

Stir together dry ingredients and add stirring until barely blended.

Add pineapple and coconut.

Bake 375° - 20 min.

Winnie's Rhubarb Muffins

1 1/4 c. all purpose flour
1 1/2 tsp. baking powder
1 tsp. salt
1/4 c. white sugar
1/4 c. brown sugar
1 1/2 c. diced rhubarb
1 large egg
1/2 c. milk
1/4 c. oil
1 tsp. almond flavouring
    white or powdered sugar for top

Mix dry ingredients.

Beat egg, add milk, oil and almond flavouring.

Pour egg mixture over dry ingredients and stir to moisten.

Fold in rhubarb.

Bake 375° - 20 min.

Dip tops while hot in sugar, or sprinkle tops with sugar before baking.

Peaches or other fruit in season are just as delicious!

Metric Equivalent Chart
For The Kitchen

1 tablespoon (tbsp.)	–	15 ml
1 teaspoon (tsp.)	–	5 ml
1/2 teaspoon	–	2.5 ml
1/4 teaspoon	–	1.25 ml
1/4 cup (c)	–	59 ml
1/3 cup	–	79 ml
1/2 cup	–	118 ml
2/3 cup	–	158 ml
3/4 cup	–	177.5 ml
1 cup	–	236.6 ml
2 cups (1 pt.)	–	473 ml
4 cups (1 qt.)	–	946 ml
		or
		.946 liters

A Great Idea for:

> showers, bridge prizes, stocking stuffers, or just an inexpensive gift for muffin lovers.

Please send me:

_____ copies of Muffin Mania at

$5.95 per copy, plus $1.00 per copy

for mailing.

Enclosed is $_____.

Name _____

Street _____

City _____

Province _____ Postal Code _____

Make cheque payable to:

> Mrs. Cathy Prange,
> 184 Lydia St.,
> Kitchener, Ont.   N2H 1W1

Or:

> Mrs. Joan Pauli,
> 553 Greenbrook Dr.,
> Kitchener, Ont.   N2M 4K5

Crumbs To Remember

Tidbits